The Fisherman
and the Fish

retold by Anne Phillips

illustrated by Loretta Lopez

MODERN CURRICULUM PRESS
Pearson Learning Group

A poor fisherman lived alone in a hut by the sea. It was a tiny hut, and the roof leaked when it rained.

Every day the fisherman went out to cast his fishing net into the sea.

One day the fisherman caught a strange fish. He was astonished by it. He had never seen one like it before. The fish was the color of the sky and the sea, and it shone like the sun.

"It would be cruel to eat such a pretty fish," he said, "so I will put it back in the sea."

3

Then the fish spoke to the fisherman.

"Thank you," it said. "I'm lucky you are a kind man and not a cruel one. I will give you a wish."

The fisherman thought.

"I want a better house," he said.

"Done," said the fish.

So the fisherman went home. He
was astonished by what he saw.

There stood a new house. The door
was green, the roof was red, and inside,
there was bread on the table for him to eat.

"How wonderful!" said the fisherman.
He sat down to eat.

Every day there was bread on the
table to eat. The fisherman did not have to
fish anymore.

But soon he got tired of bread, and he
got tired of his new house.

Back to the sea he went.

"Fish! Fish!" he called.

"What's wrong?" asked the fish.
"Don't you like your new house?"

"I want a bigger house," said the
fisherman, "and I want something to eat
besides bread."

"Done," said the fish.

The fisherman went home. He was astonished by what he saw. There sat a grand new house with stone walls and a high roof. Inside, meat was on the table.

"How wonderful!" said the fisherman as he sat down to eat.

Every day there was meat on
the table to eat.

But soon the fisherman got tired of
his meat and his grand new house.

Back to the sea he went.

"Fish, fish," he called.

"What's wrong?" asked the fish.
"Don't you like your grand new house?"

"I want a castle," said the fisherman.
"I want something besides meat to eat,
and I have a great thirst. I want
something good to drink too."

"Done," said the fish.

So the fisherman went home. He was astonished by what he saw. There stood a beautiful castle. The roof was gold and shone brightly. The doors were silver.

Inside the castle was a table with every kind of rich food and drink.

"How wonderful!" said the fisherman. He sat down to eat, and he soon lost his thirst.

Soon he got tired of his castle, though.

Back to the sea he went.

"Fish! Fish!" he called.

"Now what?" said the fish. "Don't you like your castle?"

"I want a bigger castle," said the fisherman.

"You want too much," said the fish. "Go home. Your castle is gone. Your grand house is gone. Your little house is gone. Even your hut is gone. You will have to sleep on the sand with the sky for a roof. And I think it's going to rain."

"Oh, fish," said the fisherman.
"I got greedy. I'm sorry. Please give
me back my little hut."
The fish thought it over.
"Done," it said, "but don't ask again."
"Thank you," said the fisherman.
With that, the fish was gone.

The fisherman went home.

There sat his little hut.

"How wonderful!" said the fisherman.

He was happy once again.

He was happy even when it rained.